the open-hearted job search

do what you truly want

Are you happy with what you do for a living? Is it truly what you want to be contributing to the world?

I realized some time ago that my job had stopped being what I want to do in my life. My living and my life were coming from two utterly different sets of values.

It was a time for a change, not just in what I did for money, but in my way of being. Another job search, especially one that started in my feeling of disengagement and frustration, wasn't the answer. This book is about what I found.

The process started out as an experiment; I made it up as I went, and it was wildly successful. This is my experience, and my advice to you.

Your search will look different from mine. That's the whole point.

It wasn't easy. I did a fair amount of "soul searching", which frankly felt like a bunch of neurotic floundering. *Maybe I'll quit my job and move to Hawai'i!* I'd tell myself. *What if I'm supposed to be a life coach?* I'd think. *A motivational speaker? A writer of books?*

What I landed on was this: I wanted not just a new job, but a process for finding work that came from my heart. Within a matter of weeks, I felt like the experience had changed me. And yes, I found a role with a company that felt like the perfect thing for me to be doing at the moment, and a first step on a journey towards contributing my piece to the world.

I didn't have to make a wild change of circumstance to experience this, though I might try that next. It only took a change in perspective, a waking up to see work in a way that could fit in with all areas of my life, everything I value… not to dictate or even just fund my lifestyle. It also took choice, deciding what I would not do and sticking to that.

If you're in a position where you either hate your job or are jobless, this may seem pretty nuts. It's not. In fact, without an attention-consuming job you get to dive more completely into the process of finding that dream.

Whatever time you do have to look for work, use it well. How many more days do you have left to work? Love each of them.

contents

get excited!

What do you want?

My co-active coach introduced me to co-active coaching's version of SMART goals a few years ago. It's like corporate SMART (specific, measurable, attainable, realistic and timely – don't those words sound so efficient?) goals, but not soul-killing. Co-active SMARTs are specific, measurable, accountable, resonant and thrilling. Thrilling over timely! Resonant over realistic! I love it.

Your first step is this: decide what you want to do. Make the decision based on what's resonant and thrilling more than anything else.

Talk to your heart. Ask it. What is wonderful and shiny and good about you? How would you express that through work? What does an amazing work day look and feel like?

Be a kid about this. Remember when you were 5, or 10, or 18… or last week. A time when you dreamed big. Draw pictures, if that's a thing that works for you. Use sidewalk chalk. Start keeping a notebook and listing some of these things. Make mind maps. Make flow charts. Make anything that appeals to you. Just get it out of your head and into some other medium. Make it real.

Do not, under any circumstances, take a skills assessment, sorting test, blah blah blah. It will be tempting, but don't even think "how?" yet. Imagine and be thrilled. You'll figure out how, find the union of practical and wow, in a bit.

Get excited first. It'll help your heart (or intuition, or gut, whatever you want to call your deeply feeling bits) talk to you.

Ask yourself – your deepest, gut-most feelings – these questions, and wait for a response.

- Who do I want to be at work?
- What does a perfect work day look and feel like?
- Are there parts of me getting trampled by work now? What would it look like if those parts were honored?
- Leaving aside all notions of what I "should" or "could" do, what am I pulled towards?
- What does work mean to me?

Are you having trouble hearing answers? There are many ways to quiet down and listen: meditation, physical work or exercise, soothing sounds, special places you go to, visualization. Many ways - try one or try several. I'll share a few of my favorites in just a minute.

Give yourself time to listen. Maybe a *lot* of time. It may be immediately clear, like a quiet voice in your mind suddenly being allowed to speak up. It could take days, months, even years.

It's okay to listen. DID YOU GET THAT? You are allowed to pay attention to your own dreams.

As you listen, hold on to what you learn. Let it light up your face when you imagine the future.

learning to listen

Is your heart not answering your questions right away? Maybe it's hard to listen. That's ok! These exercises will quiet other voices. Start here.

Sometimes your mind feels like a jungle – too many thoughts, sounds and distractions to count.

There are many tactics for approaching that wild thing. I like meditation.

Set an alarm for 15, 5, even 2 minutes. Sit in a relaxed position.

Rest your attention in your breathing. When thoughts come up, just notice them – no need to silence your mind, just watch it. What happens?

Now turn your attention towards work. What do you like doing right now? What do you hate?

be quiet

have fun

Many of us are inclined more towards images, sounds or movement to express our deepest selves. Thinking in words and practicalities can bog us down.

Is this you?

Just have some fun, then. This stuff shouldn't be painful.

Find an activity that feels like home and start going (whether going is a painting, a dance, listening to music, cooking a meal or fixing a car).

Take a moment while you play to ask what work would have to be like to feel this way – comfortable, in flow.

What feelings and images come to you?

go crazy

If you can't come up with any work that excites you... You may not be letting yourself say the thing that would really light you on fire.

Get crazy! What's the most outrageous and awesome thing you could want?

What's even more outrageous and awesome than that?

And more than that?

These things are all possible. Please don't limit yourself.

get some support

One of the best tools I use in my life is the help of a coach.

As you go through this process, you are going to occasionally freak out. You'll yell at yourself, think the process is stupid, be overwhelmed with joy and fear and all kinds of emotion. Job-seeking is a stressful process: no matter how awesome you make it, you're still talking about a fundamental life change. The more your heart is in play, the more keenly you'll feel what's at stake.

If your situation allows for it, I can't say enough good things about doing this process with a professional coach beside you. They're trained to help people identify what they want and decide how they want to get it. A good coach is also able to reflect back to you who you are and what you value, championing you when your confidence falters & challenging you when you squirm away from something that scares you.

Seek support. Having an open heart includes asking for help and recognizing that others are there for you.

Start simply. Acknowledge to another person that you are taking these steps. It make your action more tangible, and you more committed.

And of course, coaching is one of the things I'm happy to help you with, too.

If you don't have a professional coach, think about finding a partner, mentor, other job seeker, or even just a friend who agrees in advance to spend some time every week or two talking about this process with you.

right now

Be happy right now, through the beginning, middle and end of your search.

This is the most important thing I've learned about seeking anything, to really get into it and enjoy the search itself.

You're looking for work, for meaning, for change. Good. Have you noticed how often we as humans think our lives will be great once we have whatever one great thing we're waiting for? Don't wait for that new wonderful job to have what you want, where you want with the people you want. Have it now.

What does it mean to look for a job in a way that makes the looking itself compelling?

I suspect there's a core set of values that everyone wants to honor in their process.

- **learning** (you develop new skills or have new experiences, you discover things about yourself or others)
- **enjoyment** (the search is fun - why else would you keep at it?)
- **safety** (your self-image is not at risk from rejection, you're not in financial or physical danger)
- **balance or integration** (the job search complements your current life, or at least doesn't overload you)
- **presence** (you feel like you're really participating in the effort and experiencing the highs and lows)

Then each of us adds our own values. It's important for me, for instance, to be open-hearted and rely on my emotion and intuition. Presence for me is all about feeling, and connection with other people. Balance is all about feeling like the search itself is creative and leaves space for my artistic life.

Why think this much about what kind of job search experience you want to have? You could just start sending resumes out, or call your old manager who thought you were awesome. That whole process turns you and your next work into a bundle of keywords, skills and benefits.

Great, if you want a job based on those things. If you want real fulfillment, though, you spend a fair amount of time deciding what job you want to do, where, in what sort of place and with what sort of people.

I want you to take that a step further. Decide what kind of experience you want to have while you look for your next great work. It may be a lot like what you want from the work itself. Or not.

In either case, it will help you decide where to go, and it will give you the tools to be happy as you go. The values you articulate in this step become the map to your new destination.

Great cartographers spent years, decades even, mapping out new lands. Take your time, be open to change and ready for surprises.

Imagine the most fun you've ever had looking for something.

Was it a game of hide-and-seek? Finding an out-of-the-way landmark? Combing the beach for shells?

That experience could be a metaphor you apply to this job search. How could you create the same qualities as you look for work?

There's your exercise: write down a metaphor that appeals to you.

Draw a picture if you'd rather.

be a poet

do what matters

What do you value in life as a whole?

That question is sometimes hard to answer. One way to think through this is to brainstorm many words that you love, and identify from those what things are important.

Make a list of those things, and note next to each one how it can be honored in a job search.

I care about...	I'll honor it in my search by...

Are you visually inclined?

Draw yourself a treasure map. The X at the end is your perfect match of a job.

Where are the dragons?

Where are the luscious lagoons you want to linger by for a bit?

make maps

ask the future

Have a little chat with your imagined future self, the self you'll be when this round of seeking is brilliantly complete.

You did everything that mattered.

What does Future!You know? How did that come to be?

make it gulp-worthy

So. You're looking at a map, metaphorically or otherwise. It may change. That's okay. It's there to keep you moving and aware of your path, not to keep you locked onto a path like a trolley car. What's your first step on that path?

You might care deeply about having passionate relationships with both your work and your family. Can you involve them in your search? How might you search for workplaces that truly honor families? Maybe recognition and excitement are really important to you - perhaps you could create a dramatic, splashy way of finding work: create a YouTube video, get on the news, become an internet celebrity.

The first step of my connected search was... well, connections. Relationships. I want to feel like I belong to a community made of colleagues, one that supports individuality over any corporate identity. Once I knew how important it was to make connections and understand people (not to mention exploring what it might be like to work with them), the rest of this step seemed obvious. If you've answered the questions in Very Official Step Four, I believe your first steps will be equally obvious.

Continuing with my story! A few places sparked my sense of wonder. What would it be like to work there? What are the people like? Could the things I love be the things they love? I imagined wonderful, heartfelt conversations with others who'd turn out to be "my people". I wanted to know them.

I was also afraid to know them. Here's a secret: I'm a giant weenie. I was terrified to ask people these questions. I was fairly certain that everyone I talked to would think I was crazy at worst and at best just not understand what I was asking.

I believe the things we first think to do and stop ourselves from out of fear are usually what we want most. So I knew that this way of looking was right, just by how frightening and delightful it sounded.

You'll need to connect to people no matter how you choose to do your search. I wanted meaningful, heart-to-heart kinds of connections. So I reached out to a few people I know, with a direct and open question – do they know anyone at the companies I'd like to imagine working at? Do they know of (or work at) other places that really connect with their own hearts?

Gulp.

That was hard to say – the word "heart" in front of people I've worked with. The questions stuck in my throat, behind a veneer of "cool professionalism".

When did "professional" come to mean "emotionless"? In any case, it wasn't my idea of professionalism, and I had started to realize how much this search, for me, was now about being who I am and doing what feels good to me. I leapt. I asked the questions. I maybe looked like a dork.

It felt good to ask people for what I really cared about, and within a day several had sent me possible contacts. A few surprised me with their feelings about their own work. Unexpected results!

Some did ignore the request (possibly these folk thought I was crazy). Others hooked me up with recruiters or HR people – the kind of people who have a pre-fabricated message about their companies and aren't exactly allowed to talk to you about their personal love of work. Enough of my own people connected me with others in new, meaningful ways, though, that I had a ton of opportunities for new conversation.

This part is fun! I love getting to know new people, or getting to see a part of someone that I didn't know much about.

And that's exactly what I wanted: this aspect of looking for a job isn't drudgery. It was easy to make time for – because I wanted to be doing the work itself, not just experiencing the results in however many months. I looked forward to these conversations, and I enjoyed the surprises. It became fun-exciting more than scary-exciting.

Heartfelt connections may not be exactly the thing you seek. Maybe what will excite (and petrify) you is boldness in your self-promotion, and you need to make a viral internet video promoting your mad awesome skillz. Maybe you're all about data, and what you'd love is to find out every fact possible about your field or prospective companies.

Just ask yourself one question: *does this idea freak me out a little*?

Yeah?

That's what you're looking for on your first steps: exciting new ways to approach your search that speak to your heart. Decide what you want to ask for. Gulp, and take that step. A coach or support person can be a wonderful challenger here. If you make wimpy little commitments to yourself, that person can check you, push you for more, and push you to be honest. Then, when you make the choices that make you gulp, your support will be right with you, cheering.

just ask

If your own gentleness and determination aren't sufficient right now, don't worry. Remember that buddy you're working with?

Talk to them. Talk to your friends. Pray, if that suits you. Admit you're afraid, or stuck. Allow them to help. Let them push you & support you.

Who can you ask for help? Write down at least one name here, and commit to talk to them.

be afraid
be very afraid

If you're struggling to decide what course to take, try my way. I am great at being afraid!

What sounds really great that you "just know" you can't do?

Maybe there's an intimidating company you just couldn't talk to, a change of jobs you can't contemplate, learning something new, asking for help you're "sure" no one has time for.

That voice that assures you it's impossible isn't really you.

Can you imagine it being amazing? Does imagining it make you want to throw up a little? Yeah, you probably want to do that.

what do you fear?

Some people can leap right in – they might need to look the other way, sure, but they jump in and do it.

I have to say I'm not those people. I come up with tiny ways to test and prepare for things that scare me. I once asked 20 people I barely knew out on dates to practice not being shy. I tell myself the whole way up the mountain that it's just a test, and I can hike back down anytime I want.

It's okay to be gentle with yourself.

Everyone is afraid of some things. Take some time to think about what scares you. Get comfortable and get out a pen. Think about your commitment to change your work.

What little voices come up? What do they say? Fears may come in different forms: actions you want to take that scare you, outcomes you hope to avoid. Just write them down.

When you have a few that really make you squirm, look at those more closely: are they true? Unknown? Or even based on assumptions that are totally false?

be present, be you

Part of finding fulfilling work is being able to guess (by the way, guessing is about the best you can do for your future self – you and your circumstances will change, after all) what you'll be happy doing. Our first step on this path was thinking about the kind of work we intend to do, the things that appeal to the best parts of ourselves. You've thought about what you want, right?

The other part is what others want that you have. You also need to match yourself to what you want. That's what's next! Think about the qualities in yourself that you want people to know you have. What do you value in yourself?

You can take many different routes to decide this for yourself: making lists, talking to others, taking tests, creating art that represents your self. I am proud, for instance, of both my ability to hear and coach others - when I really pay attention - and my own passion for information gathering and sharing. Those are things I try to show when I talk to people about possible jobs.
This, knowing ourselves, is ironically one of the times we as humans most seem to need support and input from others. Go for it.

You have traits and experiences that no one else has, had, or will have. The more you think about yourself and your many wonderful qualities, the clearer you will be on what you want to show and communicate. You may also learn about the person you want to be, and find ways to communicate that.

Job seeking is a lot like dating – and neither needs to be stressful. Ultimately, both are about matching two puzzle pieces together. Some dates are a little like recruiters, even – they have a checklist of the qualities they're looking for, and you either connect with them on paper or you don't. You probably feel a little awkward on those dates, and weird talking to hiring folk who think like that. It's ok. The situation is, in fact, awkward & weird. You don't have control of the other side of the situation, but you can make sure you are clear and confident in who you are and what you want

you're awesome, admit it

But maybe you don't spend a lot of time thinking about all your wonderful skills and qualities. These practices will help in exploring and articulating what's great about you. Go ahead – I bet you'll learn something

Ask your friends and colleagues. Heck, use past performance assessments if you've worked at places that do those things. Just ask what they really appreciate, as this feedback is much more fun to give than criticism.

By the way, when you ask, ask people you trust, who really matter to you - and tell them that.

just ask

make art

What qualities do you love at work? What images come to mind when you think about your best qualities?

Collect images that bring these things to mind. Paste them into a collage.

If a collage isn't your thing, how about…

A quilt?

A scrapbook?

A dance?

A song?

A website?

What do these playful tactics show you about yourself?

get all analytical

Stuck?

Take a really good, strengths-focused self-assessment.

[Recommendation and endorsement time, here: try Strengths Finder and the VIA assessments.]

Taking the tests is nice, but taking the tests and then reflecting on what's true or not true about them is better. Be truthful – and show off a bit for yourself.

So, what did you learn?

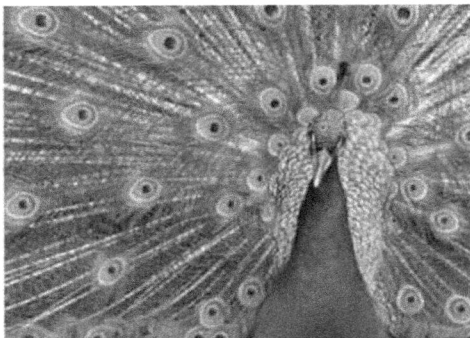

book jacket

You've been wildly successful at your dreams! Now you're about to be recognized at a banquet in honor of the soon-to-be-published secret of your success.

What will they say in your introduction? What do you want to say to your fans? Who will you thank?

And, of course, you'll want to pick out a photo for that book jacket.

writing a resume without selling your soul

I have been really good at writing resumes: clear, active descriptions of jobs that were truthful but make you sound good, using all the keywords recruiters are looking for. The resume as a sales pitch.

BORING.

It's a repetitive exercise & people get sold to so often that writing such a pitch feels soul-killing.
You're most likely to get hired as a result of a relationship you've built - not your resume. So the resume is two things: a formal introduction, if you don't know someone to build that relationship, and a way of organizing your own thoughts about your past experience and the accomplishments you value. Treat it that way - as a calling card and a communication tool.

I wanted to write a resume that tells you who I am, while still being consumable by recruiters and HR people and others who are asked to help find people to fill jobs with the shallowest possible understanding of either job or person. [Man, HR people who have to work that way? I feel for you. If you signed up for a job like that thinking it was about people & got - you know, that... there are other, better ways out there. Go toward the light.] The same basic skills – understanding the core of a piece of work, writing clearly & comprehensively – apply to a heartfelt resume, but the approach is different.

It took some mental shifting for me. I don't recommend starting with what I started with – namely, staring blankly at last year's resume on a computer screen, wondering how to take something so nicely suited to job seeking inside my company & make it both intelligible (OMG THE JARGON – I used a lot of it) and compelling (a hard job for a bulleted list of job duties). Ugh.

Once I'd finished wasting that time, I started looking around online for people whose resumes intrigued me. Be warned: there are a lot of boring resumes that serve recruiters' hunger for keywords; there aren't quite so many that give you a sense of the person behind the bullet points. Even if you – like me – are looking for a job working for someone other than yourself, pay special attention to what self-employed people write. Not having the recruiter-mindset, they tend to talk more about their authentic selves. You may see something you like.

I did this on my own search - looked through resumes and pulled out ones that spoke to me. Each of those in some way made me think *ooh, I might like you*. When I'm hiring people – usually based on resumes that recruiters have further diluted with boldfaced keywords and other detritus – that *ooh, I might like you* feeling would be like a lemonade stand on a hot summer day. It puts the feeling back in the search process on both sides – the person with a job to fill and the person who wants that job.

That's one tactic – look around for resumes that give you the feeling, since so many people post theirs online in some form. The resume you want to write from your heart probably isn't yet out in some copy-paste template (because you're not so much the copy-paste template sort of person, are you?), but you can gather collage elements that you like. What questions do others ask or answer in their resumes that connect for you? What questions do you want a client or an employer to ask you?

When you feel you have enough information collected, step away from the computer – or whatever your conventional approach is. I find hand-writing helps me be more in touch. You might work better with drawing, speaking aloud, creating little flash animations, or some other tactic. I took my notebook outside and wrote a little about each of these topics (the questions I wanted to answer for myself): what I want – which I'd already written about as I started this search, what I love to do, what I accomplished in each role, and how who I am as a person makes me awesome to work with. As you do this exercise, don't push for perfection – just let the words come out. Let your passion come out.

In addition to creating resume content, you may find that this work clarifies even further what you're seeking from a new job. That's how passion rolls – once you get it worked up, it just can't stop communicating. And I believe that's the space you want to be in when you're looking for your next big thing.

So! You've gotten structural ideas from others. You've written some content yourself. Put your content in the structure. Tada! First draft done.

I won't talk much about reviewing and refining, because those things are a breeze in comparison to what you've just tackled; if those things feel hard, find a friend who is a confident writer and ask for their editing help.

face to face

You've come to the point when you meet someone who decides whether to hire you or not. You're face to face with a job you might want.

If the hunt for a job is like dating, going to an interview is your first date. Many of us approach job seeking in general, and interviewing even more so, as a process of selling ourselves. We assume the goal is to get someone to employ us. Your heart doesn't want just any job, though - no more than you'd want a second (or fifth, or fiftieth) date with someone you had no connection with.

You can find some lousy, soulless dating advice, of course. It's common to think in terms of rules that will help you "catch" a date or a partner. You can date like you just want someone, anyone, to like you. Is that success? Someone else's approval? Not for you. Your heart wants better.

You know there's no secret formula for the perfect hot date. People are unique. Chemistry, that magical energy of connection between two people, seems to follow no formula at all. Go on enough dates, though, and you'll start to see a pattern emerge; there are three things at work: you, the other person and the space between you.

Each person is evaluating all three, looking at the connection and possibility of this relationship. The same is true in an interview. If you come in focused on you impressing them, you miss an opportunity to get to know the interviewer. You miss your own chance to assess the connection. Plus, as anyone who's seen another person do this on a date knows, you look a little bit desperate.

Whether you're just gathering information or actually seeking employment, every conversation you have is an opportunity to share, learn & decide what you want.

face to face

When you focus on your authentic self in comparison with a possible role, your experience is honest - and more fun. You get to stop thinking of "rejection" and "acceptance" and instead see connections... or not.

The interview process isn't about selling yourself any more than great dating is. It's about all three elements: you, the job, and the fit between the two. Good interviewers also recognize this, and will work to help you.

This may be a big shift in the way you think about interviewing, or it may be totally obvious. Take some time to think about it. How will you approach interviews? How will you approach people, period?

interviewing in three step
(well, four: don't forget to have fun)

learn

- Learn about the people, place and role you're considering. You get to gather hard data and make a human connection with each person you contact. Don't forget to ask questions and probe; people enjoy being listened to.

- Aim, more than anything, to have a good talk with another person. Learn about the individual you're talking to, and don't be afraid to talk about the things you have in common.

- Find out about an organization's culture before you even apply. Find contacts at places that interest you, and ask them what they care about. Get to know those people, and you'll get to know their places.

- Focus on what matters to you. Don't cram for interviews. If something about a company excites you, learn more about that, but you needn't come to an interview citing 20 reasons you fit their strategic plan.

interviewing in three step

share

- Share who you are and the skills you value. The things we repeat influence our thoughts, too - so each time you do this, you may learn about yourself or reinforce your own best qualities. That's right! Talking about your talents is good for you. Maybe as good as broccoli.

- Be ready to talk about your skills and the things that excite you. Share your passion. Admit to being good at things. Admit to not knowing. Be willing to disagree or dive into a topic with someone.

- Know there is no right answer to an interview question, only the answer that's right for you. That said, if you see your conversation partner react negatively to something you say in any other circumstance, you probably say something, or apologize. It's fine to acknowledge putting your foot in your mouth.

- Show up as yourself. Maybe slightly better dressed and a bit more polite - just as you would for a date - but still be you.

decide

- Evaluate how well the situation fits the wants and needs you've already thought through. It may even help you form a better impression of what you really want. You can think both in terms of facts and in terms of how you feel.

- Decide what's important in a job. Based on what you've decided you want and the skills you care about, what must exist for you want a job? What must you avoid? Ask questions to find out whether a job fits these musts.

- Use any tools that work for you to evaluate jobs. Pay and benefits are important, sure (you at least need to feel you're being treated fairly in order to feel comfortable in any system), but don't let that be the only thing. Does status matter? Feeling like a do-gooder? Feeling secure & cared-for? These are all ok – everyone has things they want from a job. Be honest with yourself about yours.

waiting is fine

I wrote this chapter near the end of an interview process. The company is clever, open and fun. But. They still conducted all their contemplation and decision-making in a black box. We'd have a daily exchange for a week, then they'd disappear for the next two. I was frustrated, in part because I believe that keeping in touch is a way people say they're interested. In my mind, the lack of progress updates meant someone didn't want to hire me. In this case, I thought that would suck.

You may feel like someone waiting for a call back after a third date. Is this the one? Do I want you to be the one? Why aren't you calling me? Should I call you? I called you. You haven't called? Do I look desparate? I didn't want to be with you anyhow. You suck. Please call.

There are other ways of looking at this process. People may, for instance, be embarrassed to admit they're disorganized and can't make a fast decision. Your contact may not fully grasp how decision-making works, so not have the information you want. They could be trying hard to "woo" you, and not be great at it (this is surprisingly common). You could be a second choice. Waiting without angst requires you to hold all these possibilities as equally likely - and then, to forget about them and gracefully go on with your day.

That can be hard to do. You want to stay passionate and enthusiastic about your search, yet not get overwhelmingly attached to any one outcome.

You may completely freak out, wondering what you're doing and why and if you'll ever really know what you'll be when you grow up. When you do, come back here and repeat with me: Wow. This sucks.

Sit with that for a minute. It does suck. Is there maybe something a little exciting in it? Something fun? I'm guessing it will serve you in some way. I find that a few moments after a crushing defeat, a little gleeful voice pops up in the back of my mind: Hey, I just had a Learning Experience. Cool! It's wonderful to know you're still alive and have feelings, even hurt ones. It sounds cheesy, but that's what we gain when we do the job thing from the heart.

By the way: you do know what you want to be when you grow up. Everything you are right now is enough. You're ready for this. Everyone is.

How to wait brilliantly

- Be happy. If you're enjoying the search and your life, no future possibility or lack thereof can ruin your life.

- Keep pursuing the interests that excite you. Do things that have nothing to do with work.

- You've spent time figuring out what matters to you in this process. Stick with it. Remind yourself of it.

- Be a little fatalistic. Believe that things will work out well.

- Imagine the perfect outcome. Seriously. Think about it in great detail. Be ready for it.

- Accept your worries - then pat them on the head and put them to bed.

- Wallow when you need to. It's okay to feel lousy sometimes.

it's not me, it's you

Some roles you look at aren't going to fit you. It may be obvious when you interview, or even when you first hear about them. It may not be.

This seems like an obvious thing to say, but many of us feel like every job needs to want us. Then, when the wrong jobs want us, we feel obliged to accept. Don't do that! There are jobs that sound good but are looking for something that you don't have or know. There are jobs you're wildly qualified for that aren't right for the person you are or want to be. There are perfect jobs with tragic, non-negotiable flaws.

Each of these possibilities leads to the same feeling: rejection. Yours or theirs. In an ordinary job search, you might experience hundreds of rejections, many of them impersonal letters or simple non-responses to resumes. You might reject even more possibilities - every job you don't apply to, every non-response to a recruiter who sees your resume on Monster is a form of rejection.

Searching from your heart will make you more selective and more successful (relatively). It will also make disappointment more intimate.

So. What do you do about that?

- First, of course, is feel it. Remember: Wow. This sucks. It might not even suck, exactly. It might be flattering. It might be relieving. You can feel those things, too; I hope it will only rarely flat-out suck.
- Have some boundaries. Know what you will and won't accept. You know there are some things that drive you crazy; don't tolerate those. Walk away fearlessly if you need to.
- Stick to your values, the things you want from this search. Write them on a balloon or a soft, squishy ball, and have someone throw it at you. Tape it to yourself. As important as the right job is, being the self you want completely eclipses that.
- Always be gracious in your response. Talk to the person on the other end of the decision - whether you're doing the rejecting or they are - and part kindly, with hope for their future and yours.

When you've done all those things, move on to what's next. Let the rejection go, as best you can.

Don't question your decisions or regret the past – you're the only person who knows how to be you.

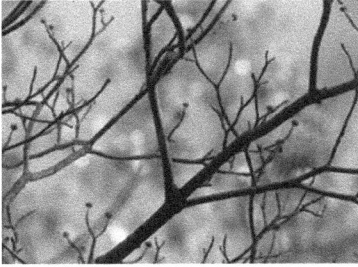

time machine

Step into your time machine. Relax and breathe easily.

It's six months from today. What has happened?
What's different? What was really fun?

Write down as much detail as you can think about – and really inhabit the future. Use the past tense to describe this job search that now, in your time machine, started 6 months ago.

Now skip forward another year. What does this year look like?

play!

This one is easy!

Do things that delight you, that light you up inside, and have nothing to do with the decision.

- Go to an amusement park.
- Get out a hula hoop.
- Make a huge feast for your family.

What can you do today to play while you wait or decide?

Give your mind a rest. You may be surprised how quickly decisions become easy.

ask the oracle

There's something exotic and exciting about asking the magical ether for answers.

Give it a shot. Consult oracles.

Try a spreadsheet of pros and cons.

Try a tarot reading.

Read your horoscope every day.

Ask a five-year-old.

Flip a coin.

Here's the secret: none of these things give you clear answers, and it doesn't matter if you "believe in" them. You'll respond, you'll fill in the details, and then you'll know (the answer you had all along).

decisions, decisions

Here's a funny story about my job search: my job and I rejected each other the first time around. We came to one point that neither of us could negotiate on, parted amicably, and I figured it was over. A month later, the perfect outcome I'd imagined in detail came to pass, in the form of another offer - and it was just the right one. No matter what other jobs were under consideration, that was the one I wanted. I just knew.

You will, eventually, need to make decisions about what you want to do. All the work you've just done from that lovely heart of yours will pay off - probably in ways you can't even imagine as you start off down this road, incomplete map in hand. Those surprising discoveries are part of the fun.

Know this, when that sexy little job offer is in front of you: you did this. You made it happen.

You don't really need advice about what to do when the right thing happens. You already know. No amount of process or logic can outsmart that feeling of rightness. Say yes. Savor it. Get ready to grow.

Enjoy your life.

hi, there.

I'm April, from Rise Up Work. Now that we've spent this time together, you might want to know a little about me.

I'm a blogger, a consultant, a dancer, a coach for individuals and teams. Most of all, I care about people, all of us, finding the work that suits, soothes and nourishes us.

I owe some people thanks, too.
- My coach, Heather Jelks of Nautilus Coaching, for being here through this and every awesome process.
- Photographer Tara Donaldson. She took these pictures of me. I love them! She also took many of the photos I used throughout this work to help you take a breath and get inspired.
- My parents & my sweetheart – who, when I suggest things like "I'm going to start the next workforce revolution, and everyone's going to be happier!" think that sounds like a great idea.

Thanks especially to you for reading, and for daring to want something new and great in your work. I hope this process works brilliantly for you!

Tell me how it works out for you. You can find me on www.riseupwork.com and email me at april@riseupwork.com.

www.ingramcontent.com/pod-product-compliance
Lightning Source LLC
Chambersburg PA
CBHW032021190326
41520CB00007B/568